endings

bruce

bisset

Earl of Seacliff Art Workshop

ISBN 978-1-86942-225-7

Published by: Earl of Seacliff Art Workshop

P O Box 42, Paekakariki, 5034, Aotearoa New Zealand

Email: olearymichael154@gmail.com

Web Site: http://michaeloleary.wordpress.com

Sales / Distribution: Write at it Productions

417 Whitehead Rd Hastings 4122 Aotearoa New Zealand

Email: booksalesnz@gmail.com

Also available via Amazon.com in e-pub format

© **Bruce Bisset 2024**

Website: brucebisset.com

This book is copyright. Apart from any fair dealing for the purpose of private study, research, criticism or reviews, as permitted under the Copyright Act, no part may be reproduced by any process without the permission of the publishers.

Cover photography/design: **Petra Zoe**

Contents:

Foreword by David Eggleton   pg. 1

Poems (in ~ chronological order) pg. 4

Songs (with basic chords)   pg. 108

Endword by Bruce Bisset   pg. 119

About the Author   pg. 121

Dedicated to all the friends who have slipped away over the years.

Foreword

Bruce Bisset is a rock'n'roll poet who never sold out. Starting back in the 1970s he hung in there with his poetic licence, a beret-wearing barfly bard who came up hard. And though he stopped performing for a few years, he never stopped writing. Gruff and bluff, growly and resonant, with a certain shaggy-dog humour, he operated outside the mainstream. Bruce has always remained his own man, with any stage as his space to recite his verses to the people.

Bruce began writing and performing when poetry was on the up and up, taken off the page and put onto the stage by the likes of Sam Hunt, Hone Tuwhare, Gary McCormick, Jon Benson, myself, and others. Bruce became one of those poetic declaimers who got their act together and took it out on the road, touring constantly up and down the land. Poetry got crowds going back then, part of the groundswell that emerged from grass roots or flax roots movements in the late twentieth-century, when poetry was getting itself everywhere as a vehicle for people with something passionate to say and saying it in poems on street corners, in pubs, cafes, university student quadrangles and at rock festivals.

Bruce Bisset came to national prominence at the Nambassa Festivals of the late 1970s, a shamanistic voice channelling thoughts and attitudes and emotions that spoke to the moment when things in New Zealand were being shaken up and society was changing. The old order represented by Muldoonism was voted out in 1984, which is when this collection begins.

Endings is ordered chronologically like a diary and presents a selection of work taken from four decades of poetic output. It's a kind of memoir in verse creating a narrative arc out of the poet's life-story that traverses Aotearoa through time and place, providing facets of this poet's view of the world. As an autobiography it is philosophical, wry, irreverent, shrewd and down-to-earth. Like a good keen bloke from way back, Bruce Bisset tucks poetry under his arm and runs with it, swerving away from body-tackles, towards the try-line. He pricks pretention and celebrates the everyday with one eyebrow raised and with many quips and asides.

It's true though that his poems really are written for performance. Written down, they spell out the performance of his life and times. W.B. Yeats said that out of the quarrels with others we write polemic and out of the quarrels with ourselves we write poetry. Endings runs the gamut from his beginnings as an audacious buccaneer of the spoken word to the quieter, more ruminative and self-reflective poet of recent times as he takes stock of his life's journey.

There's always been a spiritual need for poetry out in the community, but poetry itself has many constituencies, answering to the various needs and requirements of different groups. Some like their poems obscure and artful, playing games with language and metrical formulas and deferential to the traditional canon. Others prefer their poems to be clear, transparent, obvious perhaps, but also heartfelt, and speaking a language they can recognise and endorse.

The poems in Endings are often confessional, running the gamut of emotions and telling it as it is, or isn't. They are accessible and immediate rather than esoteric and baffling. Bruce Bisset is no baffler. He uses poetry to speak his truth as someone from the school of hard knocks. The poems are there to be chanted in the key of life.

Joseph Conrad reckoned everyone must walk in the light of his own heart's gospel and swear by that. Endings shows a poet doing so. There are poems about masculinity, about relationships: lover/partner, father/son. There are poems about domesticity: babies becoming children becoming young adults, then grown-ups. There are poems about long-gone travelling companions, such as the musician Ralph Bennett; and poems about Vietnam War veterans, poems about partying hard and about catching the Waiheke ferry. Cantankerous to a degree, concerned with dissent and protest, other poems and poem-songs take us from the destruction of the Mangaweka Viaduct to the climate emergency of the Takaka floods, from the Covid-19 pandemic to the attack on Parihaka, to protests over Palestine and the razing of Gaza by the 'Israelites'.

Prayer is a kind of tune which all things hear, said the poet George Herbert. The same might also be said of poetry. Bruce Bisset speaks in tune and often that tune is the blues, but not always. He wants his poems to filter through as simply as possible, communicating directly. The American poet John Crowe Ransome wrote that: 'The poet perpetuates in his poetry an order of existence which in actual life is constantly crumbling beneath his touch.' There's a sense of that in Endings :

> i let the weight of the world
> drop away
> and my soul
> is nourished.
>
> this is what i need, i realise
> : nature, lightness, calm :
> i have lived beyond despair
> and now
> wish only to heal
> myself.

-- David Eggleton, Dunedin, 2024

POEMS

    put it on a postcard

i couldn't believe it

i could not believe it

they took the fucking viaduct away

the bloody wrecker

was so cocky he

left his mark upon it:

you've got a lot to answer for, Ron

: and the railway lines

weren't where they always are:

good thing no trains were coming.

and Ralph gave the last rites

to the redbarn landmark

"shame Rita Angus is dead," he said

"sure to be gone soon."

right now, the sign still says

M A N G A W E K A

but it looks like a tombstone

: rest in peace.

                              March 84

a Taranaki poem

slowly, through the screens of my inheritance
i learn of my country:
standing with the pulse of the land
vibrating up into my feet
travelling the riven rock river of Taranaki's trail
remembering Parihaka in
an Eltham centenary advertisement that states
"the honour of being the first settlers..."

somewhere near here the spirit moved

> *ah, but the white man*
> *would take your symbol for cowardice*
> *mock any power not made of iron*
> *conceal your home from your eye*
> *leave tokens and*
> *the count of the dead*
> *as a blessing*

Te Whiti you were forged too pure to learn
that peaceful protest only succeeds
when you are the same race
when it is backed by power that can threaten the state
when the world can hear your words

nowadays few Maori live east of the mountain
little wonder
with the rape completed
it must almost be time
for his return

March 84
originally published in The Globe Tapes (Hard Echo Press, 1985)

knowing what present to buy

we have a disagreement about nothing

she wants me to sleep in case i'm tired

i want her to have some hours in a roomy bed

besides, as she wouldn't understand now

fathers need preparation time too

: she's just broken

her favourite handmirror

the one in the wooden frame

with a little silver shield

on the back:

i've made up and consoled her

sat down to take space and

run out of typewriter ribbon

: now she's drifting off to sleep

– i hope, with the contractions

at 8-10 minutes – may be the baby

will be born around 6, maybe around 10

and this will seem

so much trifle, then.

June 7 88

back to by the motorway

now he cuts his teeth
two at a time
and is brave, but still
drives an edge
through the day:
a week ago
driving through a Takaka flood
we were safe bar the torrents
of Nature: here
often the family is jarred
by the torrents of man
and when his gums shriek
there is noise and bedlam
inside as well as out.
calmly, it seems, almost serene
we battle amongst it
but i would gladly accept a lift
four hundred miles away.

Jan 4 89

what to do after work

thomas wants a bounce? oh look hon, bouncey, bouncey
here you hold your rattle
do you want it? that's a boy
what's this squeaky thing? listen, squeaky, squeaky
let's see you pull this string
and it plays Brahm's lullaby
oh, you'd really like some dinner? well,
we've got peach and banana
with your favourite kumara
and some tit to wash it down
now we'll put you on the floor
and watch while you roll over
and eat daddy's newspaper
and squirm yourself around
ouch! tom, that's a beard
yes, argh! yes, daddy makes a noise
no, it's not one of your toys
and i've never liked Brahms
here then, let's go walkies
we can take the dogs, go for a walk
yes dogs, down girls, yes tom, that's
just the way good doggies are

and oh, the trees the leaves the flowers
feel the wind on your head in your hair
see the cars go zzoom by

see the children playing and
the branches swaying and the
wavelets breaking on the old stone stair

and back home, yes, back to mummy
hello mum! and laugh and cry
have a bath and some more titty
then to bed, we hope, goodnight!

oh he's woken. oh damn, sorry.
change the nappy, clean the mess
give him cuddles and caresses
finally to sleep, quick!
we've just got time
to get some rest.
who says babies aren't beautiful?

Nov 22 88

"offer up your best defence"

i feel alone:
i've spent the afternoon
cleaning house, counselling a friend
in need, and now, while
my bath runs, i write
to you
: and am lonely.

contemplating an affair, wondering
if you plan one too
will dinner in town with friends suffice
or must sex complete the evening:
i've trusted you this far, but now
when i'm no longer sure i trust
myself, i wonder.

and the radio plays that song that says
"this is the end of the innocence", and i
am inclined to agree
: if i venture out tonight
i may find
it might well be.

and at other times, many times, lately
thoughts like these
make the sadness sadder

make the dreams to dust

make life again a series of

hard choices, where once

i believed we could have roses

forever.

well, not quite that idealistic, but

you know what i mean. ah well, i'll go

and soak my poor tired soul

try to make-believe the right things

push away the anger and the cold

and pretend in bed

as i read myself to sleep

i'm not worried.

Oct 31 90

here we are on waiheke

i am approached to contribute
some trifle to a book
that, combined with pictures, will
leave impressions of this island.
i'm at a loss: looking
through the past 8 years
two fat folders yet
so thin
i wonder how a third that time
has passed here. and where
its record might lie.
not that i'm
complaining
i've only myself to blame if
months slip by with no words
to memory them
and it's not lack of interest
nor intent that holds them in:
i just never seem to get around
to picking up a pen.
perhaps i'm busy

Sept 21 91

last night i tried to write
a love poem for you
but the lines refused to flow
and all i got was a headache. it's
been with me all day.

it's not that i don't want to, or that
(of course) i don't love you
it's not even that i can hate you
it's just the way it is.

and you'll say you get the worst of it
and you're right, because
that's the way poets often work
actions to strive for the good times
words to describe the bad
: but you don't value either, from me.

people say it's a learning curve
and experience shows us the way
but the slope i'm travelling along now
goes downhill day by day
and whether you're pulling from the bottom
or pushing from the top
it's a sure bet for disaster
down love's long drop.

i'm trying to write a love poem for you
but the love won't come
and i'll cry myself to sleep tonight
and you won't care.

perhaps you don't deserve it.

Feb 24 92

how carelessly we use words:
one unthinking statement
and the damage is done
: i remember
coming home after a shitty day
to my wife and newborn son
"i've never been happier" she said and i
snarling, growled "i have"
and hit the fridge barely noticing
the effect the way she drooped the sad
let-down i'd delivered, all unaware
unintended, insensitive - just
a typical reaction to
a not so marvelous working grind and
this little thing it was
that broke our love.

i've tried to erase it, but
once new light is shed
i guess no-one ever quite sees someone
in the same glow again.

"turn on your hot light
in the middle of a young boys dream..."

she did, and i turned it off again.

March 10 92

how do i tell you i love you

in words that make you feel you

love me; how do i say

you're all my life, now

and for the future

when for you the future is

tomorrow; how do i make

a little seem a lot, a look become

a caress, a smile a warmth and

a touch a heart-held greeting;

how do i bring you near

and let the tenderness inside

enrobe you, dear; and how

can i wrap this bitterness, this hatred

anger and fear

all up in a parcel and send it

to the farthest place from here...

how do i tell you i love you

when you will not hear.

early 92

after dropping you back to the ferry

this used to be where the heart was
now it's just a house:
pink walls, bare floors, and all.

you think i don't know how you felt:
you're wrong.

i guess i was making a pressure point for myself
for us
thinking, if she concedes to my plans
we'll be fine; if not
then it's time to lose.
and maybe the way it's worked out
that was the correct thing to do.

but without you here, without tom
coming home is
like putting out the rubbish:
something you just do,
that somebody takes away
: no heart in it.

now
i'd leave tomorrow if
it would really change things
but it won't. seems
we were both right
and this may be best, after all.

but like my heart, this house is empty.

April 11 92

waiting (part one)

meanwhile, my boy is laughing growing
away from me, having
others watch him learn
talk about the world
to him its all the same, really
if dad has a substitute like
some old lover she dredged up
for no better reason.
i miss his cheeky smile
his exclamations of joy
even his frown
. an empty bedroom
teases me
speaks in memory, so
i don't go in
when he's not around.
somewhere there
apparently
is everything he needs, almost;
and i have declined
to opt for war, rather
a sad forgiving peace
: in the hope that some day
he will catch me unawares and rush
to my arms as though there never were
a parting.

and we will laugh and grow

Nov 4 92

wildflowers

those jumbo jets of the forest

the kereru have eaten

all the ripe loquats

the wildflowers and

the bottle-brush bloom and

tui come to drink

their nectar, as

i would your sweetness, but instead

pass on these fragile tokens so

you may keep their colour

and purity intact

and think of me thinking of you

in some other garden

October 1993

for PJ

ralph

i think of you
at odd times
remind myself i haven't
written/rung since
you separated, wonder
why that is ...
roads spent
and i listen
for the first hour in a long while to
that tape we made the weekend the photo
that hangs on my bedroom wall was taken
smile at the old youthful sounds
reminisce that we were
compatriots, comrades, but
... friends? i don't know
if i can answer that;
not in the sense
traditionally felt
(i suspect) ... and is that the reason? or
is it something deeper, within, like
my desire to hit those streets
again and be
that someone who could always travel
at your side, and live
one evening at a time, oddly.

well, that's another day gone.

April 27 94

waiting for a cab

the penguins don't nest
in the rocks by the wharf anymore:
the changes and
the crowds have driven them away
the jazz singer thinks he might have
to go too: perhaps the Barrier - at
least he can fly
(a Piper)
: and young aesthetes
pen lyric social commentaries
weekly, in the local paper
and greet the waves from the back
of silver-grey Mercedes
: when it comes, driven by a moonlighting policeman,
there's a dial for everything
and they're all down the middle:
battery, water, fuel, revs, speed, temperature, time - all
a bit after 10, into the eleventh hour
we go, and hey
they say animals sense quakes early, don't they.

March 21 95

giving favours

election time
and i'm kissing babies
: he smiles seeing
his mum and dad together leaning
over him, oohs
with pleasure, gives
a little wave as if to say
that's nice, that's what i like
and we kiss and cuddle and feel
together.

you always take the hard route
she says
and this is one:
going home to be alone without my family.
and i may be broke and losing votes
but life keeps right on growing
: it's the bonus you least expect
and value most.

the world may say many things, or nothing
about any one of us
but the treasures of the soul will always last.
when you balance up the things they tell about me, boy
i trust there'll be no doubt for whom
your ballot's cast.

but just in case, remember daddy's kiss:
a simple gift to win us heart to heart.
and when you have its meaning
in the larger world to come
you'll know, despite it all, i played my part.

in love, with love, for love of brennan
brennan angus william bisset hill-rennie

Sept 28 95

one two three four

i know a few vets:
some i count as friends.
i never ask about the war
: they never tell me.
25 years is a long time
to keep silent.

inside it's a realmare that
wakes you in the night, panting
hard enough the wife can only
softly touch and whisper nothing
much as it seems over come
it's anguished rage just waiting
to explode
: like it was
: like it is.

i never ask: it's written
just behind the skin, within
each muscle, sinew and bone
all jumping, etched
the stigmata of modern madness peering
from some sideways place just
behind the eye, the edge
of vision creeping
up and wanting to be told.

they never tell: the good ones struggle
through their smiles with family and friends
build hideaway retreats in bush with
views over the open, keep
dogs as playful pets and treat
their children well. the bad
do everything the same, except
maybe workout a little more
on the downstairs homegym, maybe

stay from the public's gaze a little more when wariness
sets in, maybe
dress up once every blue moon and
get out the souvenirs and go
sliding through the foliage at
the bottom of the garden
looking for targets.

there's only one movie playing, a hit cult
: and it's there on video, with all the colours extra bright
even after all this
anytime. i know why the silence lasts:
the soundtrack is too loud for us to hear
and you wouldn't inflict it on anyone
not already on tape.
that's why the job never ends:
be cool gets a whole true meaning.

i know a few vets ...
hey, but i'm only guessing.

Oct 28 95

    shells

battlesmoke sky
tinfoil sea
a boy
        a rock
                a ripple

dinghy drifting
floating free
what
        am i
                a riddle

redhat laughter
calling me
there
        his life
                a giggle

my hereafter
coloured be
greyed
        i smile
                a little

                            Shelly Beach August 98

this crazy kaleidoscope
this life:

when it all unreels
at the final moment will i think, "not bad".

despite the aches, despite
bitter regrets

the joys the sheer exhilaration
of those times death was cheated

the loving and the violence and
the too strange days

the grubby secrets carried
beyond the grave

the forlorn hopes of futures
in a child's eyes

the sheer confused enormity
of it all.

this crazy kaleidoscope, this life:
weigh well the gift against the price

June 6 03

thoughts while she's away

hot summer nights
music wafting across the water from
the other side of the bay
changing from rock to spacey keyboard as
the night-mist closes down around
1 am: hot as hell back-stage, tonight
as we reel off the penultimate
show of the season: lots
of young things in next to nothing
baring their fannies in the dressing room, giving
old fellas like me
more heat to handle; i take off
as soon as i might after the show, home
to an empty house crowded with
the bric-a-brac of two people in
the throws of moving together, not quite
enough space yet in the lounge to
swing a pussy, but at least the office – once
a bedroom – is ready and i'm here, keeping
mind and fingers busy while
the music drifts and the maidens
dance in memory and
i try to be sedate and responsible and not
get myself into any more trouble. shit, and you know
the worst part about it
is i even enjoy
letting the world go by these days, these
hot summer nights made
for young and young at heart and i
am neither any more.

out to pasture? well at least
i have an island paradise to graze on
if the rebel soul is tamed and trapped and
well tempered then so
be it. i've
had more than my share of flings and
nights when neither temperature
nor music nor for that matter age mattered.
if i choose to be sedentary now, so what? i
have no regrets. if only
the little demon way in back
would shut the fuck up and stop
nagging, life would be just dandy.
wouldn't it.

                                              Jan 14 00

happy happy

our boy, the injury from his new bike's crash forgotten,
dances on the deck in the gathering dark
delighting in the last
of the cascades and sparklers left
over from Guy Fawkes as
we welcome the New Year, and
the full moon rises ponderous and orange
over Palm Beach

"let's hope it's a good one for us," says the wife
and we allow ourselves a hopeful smile
and wish our son goodnight;
but while she puts him to bed i
stare at the face of our neighbour and
cannot help but think it sad and anxious
: if this is god hiding as
he watches
he has much to trouble him.

i do not like to read omens:
i did
far too much of that as a youth
and look where it got me. but the world
is divided in far more fundamental ways
today than back when we only
had A-bombs and Cold Wars to fear about.
for or against
the Pax Americana or
the idolaters of a dubious freedom
: this century may prove more wasteful than the last
and the paranoiacs right.

ah, me. not rich enough to celebrate carefree despite
not blind enough to do the slave shoe shuffle drunk
too sane mature and haunted for
my own good.

and yours?
well, if the moon's face is anything to go by
it'll be an edgy time.
cheers!

				Dec 31 01

bombarded

a whole new century folks! wait for it
bigger and better than the last
even more war! even more terror! even more
global rapaciousness coming
NOW to a home like yours

see it on 47 channels! experience it live! nothing
quite beats the adrenalin rush of the corporate junkie bombardier
lining you up
for another hit

and
for just one dollar a day
you too can salve your conscience
and keep the munitions rolling with
the rest of your average wage
feed the starvelings enough to live
til the next round of
explosives fall
: make those twin towers count!

my word, we're cooking
with or without gas now! and when
they're democratised to hell lets
grab the windfall
gm the crops and dig the oil
cart off those profits, folks, for the next great campaign!

save the world? oh yes we're
saving the world for freedom
saving the world for peace
saving the world for brotherhood

saving the world for ourselves

don't let those leftie blackman greenie mullahs tell
you otherwise!

roll up! roll up! seats are limited
and emptying fast! don't miss
our all new exciting episodes
here, in the century of progress

March 18 02

just do it

when i was younger
i was a complete bastard
: i didn't mean to be, it wasn't planned
wasn't malicious intent:
i simply didn't know what my actions meant.

why? because i was exploring life
i had to find out
i wanted to know what this whole thing is about
: to wallow in experience, gorge
on sensuality
stimulate each organ and
expand my own reality:
selfish, egocentric, nihilistic and debauched
: a bastard, sure: i was young.

yet: it seemed to me i knew what life was for ...
now i find i am not certain any more.

i do not glory in revels
instead debate inanities
i do not gaze in wide-eyed wonder
but weep for humanity
i do not forceful prance
but question my sanity

is this wisdom? they say
knowing you are nothing is the start, a perspective
which age giveth
: i'm not so sure.
perhaps the young inherently know
what we older ones choose to ignore

or forget.

that life is in a moment, is a marvel, is transient
is to be taken whole, not chewed on til its rancid
is to feel and cry and shout and die
as chance makes it.

is not to think, but to be
to overflowing.

anarchic? superficial? what are these
but concepts jaded by the old upon the young
meaningless? lacking fulfilment? how make such claims
when the essence of excess is to have fun?
if laughter is the medicine of life
then age cuts it off like a knife.

the natural inclination to bastardry is unfortunate, true.
but i enjoyed every second of it. didn't you?

                                                                  Sept 17 03

"Uneven Surface"

says the big orange sign outside my door
warning every casual passerby
it's a road full of pratfalls and pretensions, son
lots of lows amongst the highs
black holes and ruts, blocks and bridges and such
to skew the unwary wheels of life as it rolls by

yeah, uneven surface - what better
summation of the poet's way
not to put too fine a point on it, it's
just the sort of phrase to hold me in sway
pin me in as if proclaiming "look
here's a good dog had his day"

uneven, on the surface
of things you'd agree i'm sure
twenty years between books and no-one
within hearing asking more
and these thrown-up bits by chance related
less a treasure, more a chore ....

while underneath the macadam the rocky substrate grates
and heaves with every heavy load that 'pon its black top weights
and like old bones doth grind and growl and curse the seven fates
that make such choice as art or life without art's sake

uneven
        yeah, that's it
rent and wounded and not even yet kerbed
rubbed away and tar-patched up and not
given what measure is deserved
and only once in the odd blue moon
faint recognition of past services observe

so bring out your steam-rollers your asphalt and your trucks
scrape me up and smooth me over, and bury me in my luck
and pass unseeing by no sign that aims to arrest you at the crux
and at the speed of progress from the breast of torpor suck

                                                    Aug 18 03

last time home

funny how even
the gladwrapped vines of Te Whau
or the quarry-scarred end of Stoney Ridge
seem wistfully welcome in
this moody February's evening light
: the massed mounded hills greening
the space between quiet
sea and storm-gathered sky: the
city towers lost in smog-haze behind.

is this my last time here for a while?
yes, and here's
a bellicose walking contradictionary
lambasting me on principle in
the local rag; a friend
wanting to go with us and suggesting
we can keep in closest touch by webcam; two
laughs in quick succession. ah, Waiheke.

well of course i'll miss it. it's
the place i came to be
until i die
: my son has altered the script. they
do that, don't they?

perhaps dying isn't an option any more.

later, computer booted, lone dog yapping somewhere
in the full moon dark across the bay
wife and child asleep

as usual, i think
about the list i'll start tomorrow: a million
things to do in just 10 weeks, and then
another ferry ride
but this time leaving.

i shall try to be joyful in the interim.
in this place, thank and despite all, that's
still
not so hard.

Feb 6 04

    moved

here i am
stuck in a box
inside a box
inside a box
called the Hawke's Bay:
free to smoke myself to death.

the view
through the windows that don't
open far enough for me to escape
is a couple of small trees
part of the side of the house
and a glimpse of asphalt street
: totally inspiring.

this place
raised from the dead
set in primeval ooze
sucks at the soul:
how
people grow here
i have no idea.

things do.
fruit vines veges animals
: not people, surely
not people. yet
outside somewhere there are artists singing
folk of good heart labour
to educate my son and
he and that is the reason we're here.

i don't yet understand this contradiction. how
a flowering of spirit can come
from a dearth of inherent good. how
people can rapturise about nature

when the nature of the people-places
is akin to prison.

how
the ongoing rape of what can grow
is consented, as if
it is simply how things must be.

schizophrenia? perhaps. anyone
going to what euphemistically is called
the beach here could
be driven to that conclusion:
shingle instead of sand.

hard place. hard edges beneath
a civil veneer.
i will have to adjust my brain. 90 degrees, for this morning
venturing out of my box briefly to test
the sunshine, i found
east where south should be.

ah, that's how they do it. switch
perspective, and then
call it friend.
hmmm.
i don't know if i'm adaptable enough for that task.

May 6 04

i don't know why my children should love me:

father's day, and each
in his or her own way
makes me feel special, when
i'm sure i've no right to be. my daughter
whom i'm lucky to see
once a year, sends me
the sweetest card – bought, but embellished with
her stars and flowers … together with a lotto ticket – while
my second son, whom
i hardly ever seem to play with (though
he's right here with me all the time) makes
his own … a cover
of symbolic lines and colours and inside
a picture of me painting, proudly
finished with his new-learned joined-up writing. and buys
a computer magazine with his own money (and without prompting)
for a present.
my eldest, a teenager whom
i've not been able to rear since
four, at least calls
and asks solicitously after my health. all
good stuff, eh? all loving. all
far too kind.

: for i feel as if i'm failing them, somehow, just
by being me.

and, diminished as i am these days, i can't help
but wonder how much more cherished i
could be were i the man i'd like to think i might have been.

thank you, my children.
for letting me know
there's still some worth in this wounded soul.

Sept 6 05

striving to live
an extraordinary life in
an ordinary way
i met you
striving to live
an ordinary life in
an extraordinary way
you met me
: extraordinarily ordinary \
ordinarily extraordinary
: equals
love

March 28 05

the message the moment

raw as
word is
writing us
poems are

not what you'd expect
not as comfortable as you'd like
impossible to predict
what you're driven by

rejection
envy
wonder
rage

love
confusion
empathy
death

and when you've shed a tear
and when it all resolves
when your time is near
words dissolve

Feb 7 06

come back

there was a time when i
could get equal billing with Sam Hunt
my name on posters at festivals
appear with any of the country's
top bands, and be
well paid for it

could make hardouts laugh at my wit
hold crowds of thousands
spellbound in my hand
stop a pub to listen
even mid-drunk on a friday night

those were powerful charms

i have not forgotten how
even if the half-way dead who were
my audience
have forgotten me.
 but can i speak
this voice to the new?
Sam has a treasury of enduring presence
i have 20 years in another skin
: i remember it all
but know not where to begin.

Dec 31 06

brothers

when i was younger
i played with my brothers, laughing
together and seeing in them
no difference. what i did not see
was how hard they must have had to work
to hide their differences from me.

now i watch my brothers walk
with their colours and their difference displayed
for all to see, and
when they laugh i wonder at
the teeth within the smile. they do not work so hard
to hide that.

i imagine that i know
where they come from, where
they might go, but
it's guesswork laid upon the memory
of children.

Jan 14 07

our third winter here
and finally the roof is fixed; then
in the first rain for 40 days, my relief
is washed away by the river down the lounge wall
: fortunately nothing a good sealant and a soaking can't fix.
later, almost bedtime, another drip appears coming through
from where i cut the iron back to put
a window in the boy's bedroom upstairs. it's not serious, though, so
i throw a bucket at it and retire.
old houses, eh?

it's fortune too the rain's not heavier first up
else the drought that's cracked the land all round would cause
water to slough off in torrents, and we'd
be in danger of flooding. well, not us maybe, but the bay
in general. it's too denuded
to hold itself together
so slips are likely.
old methods, eh.

fortunately you can fix the land if you know what you're doing
though it's not as simple as a house: the drips
are not always obvious, and after
too many generations people forget what needs to be done. even
those cockies who claim to be up with the play
only seem to grasp half the story:
they might plant trees, but the soil's
still slowly dying.
much the way of the world, i expect
now the crisis is upon us
: we'll rush around doing patch-up jobs without
properly addressing the issues, and
because we're such greedy bastards we'll
be washed away in a downpouring of
our own making.
and whatever comes next
may look back at us and shake its head and wonder.
old race, A.
time for plan B.   June 10 07

dishonesty

little by little
i become dishonest
changing a word here
breaking a sentence there
diminishing the purity of the expression

i kid myself its better this way
and that it is only
age and fatigue
at falter
and certain there's enough of that

but the truth is, the force
no longer speaks clear to me
no longer rushes through, wringing out
as it should
no longer drives me on that journey
between madness and destiny
hope and belief
sureness and narcissistic indulgence.

i am at best a pallid shadow
a waning moon-faced effigy of
the burning flame of my creation that
i brought so readily to life
when i was

so i tinker, to try
to paper over the lines
spreading like varicose veins throughout
this work in progress.
and console myself it's for
the sake of my inheritance, when really
all that's done behind is best, and
the doors into true perception are all but closed.

i begin to appreciate
how a zombie must feel;
the flesh moves, shakily, but the spirit
is fled.

                                                                                     July 26 09

A Capital Party Weekend

driving out of Wellington
ahead of a storm
the clouds flowing flat out across the sky
the waves assaulting the rocks
beside the road
Kapiti Island wreathed
in mist
: best to be clear.

two days of conference chat and
consensus argument has
worn my poor brain thin; greens
getting together on policy matters is
both fun and frustration. still,
progress of sorts: a framework to take forward
for next year's local elections
: if anyone is interested, that is.

very much leavened by
the football, as in soccer: there's nothing
quite like the precious snapshot moment
of a winning goal to
produce a roar i'm sure was heard
the other side of the strait.

not that i made the stadium; prevaricating
in a search for better seats left me
stunned by the fast sell-out, and cursing
to be bereft in town at the time. but the mood
was buoyant, and every bar
had the biggest screens they could hang, and so
in the end it was almost the same

: every ooh and ahh and cheer and groan
echoed down every lane.

and the way the crowd drummed and danced and whooped
alive in the streets after the game
made me recall what i liked most
about the capital and
its denizens. nowhere else in godzone does
a public party quite like that.

back in the office with my shades to hide
the unfortunate glare of the flouros, i
tried to ignore the grins and banter
of those lucky few who'd had a freebie
the night before, and forced through
(almost a revenge) one document of three
i'd made priority.

so it worked out, you see. the football
the party
and me.

Nov 15 09

nirvana

i am going through a process of forgetting
forgetting language
forgetting people
forgetting life. one day
i will forget to breathe
my heart forget to pump
my skin to feel, and then
the world will forget me
as i will have forgotten it.

things that once
seemed of vast import are now
scratches outside the door of memory. words
that held all the wonder they could not contain
are now
useless bits of flotsam
on a sea of white.
links
that should have been
my history
are crumbled to smoker's ash.

one day
i will forget myself entire
and then i can rest.

Jan 29 09

the strangest cat (a children's rhyme)

my cat is black, and his eyes are yellow
he looks alright, but he's a very strange fellow

for a start, his tail is as bushy as a brush
his fur is long and fine – but no, don't touch!

for he hates to be patted, and if you try
you'll find his claws sharp as the sharpest knives

and as for his habits, did you ever hear
of a cat that won't eat fish – he leaves it sitting there!

and when the moon is full, he runs up and down the stairs
and hides under the table, to catch you unawares

he bosses all the neighbour's cats – he's never lost a fight
and even dogs walk well clear – especially at night

and if you call him "naughty cat" and lock him in a room
he'll suddenly be on the roof, meowing at the moon!

he does however earn his keep, by hunting rats and mice
he leaves their tails as presents for us – not very nice!

but as black and bad and feisty as this foxy cat may be
we wouldn't swap him, cause he's still part of our family

and sometimes, when the fire is warm, he'll pad in through the flap
and pretend he's not that strange at all, and curl up on your lap.

May 28 09

a rock and

i do not readily acknowledge
those who are close to me
in spirit
: at least, in more than passing:
which perhaps is why i have
so few friends of any standing.

unlooked for i receive
a gift from one who
is mayhap closer kin than most:
touched, as much by
the weight of ages it contains as by
the beautifully precise poem that
accompanies
i marvel that
i do not let my heart be plucked more often.

and wonder whether it
is only my own dream that has faded
or if the sad apprenticeship of
the human condition is
mortified against what
we might more simply gain.

July 7 10
thanks Mitch!

coffee-table cut-outs

i leaf through a book
of our left island paradise
its pictures capturing a time
of idle between idyllic
and idolatry, and sadden
at the pang that comes from knowing
things will never be the same.

a month or so back, i travelled north
and spent a day catching up
with the place. and
for the first time since leaving
it did not immediately feel like home when i stepped ashore.
the dog
was nonplussed too.

still, between the ferry and Ostend i managed
to pass a dozen hours greeting talking laughing sighing with
friends acquaintances and passers-by, who
all took me for one of their own. and as
we rattled back to Matiatia in the rather flash new bus that came along
the cool of the winter's night
offered an easy blessing; a cloak of acceptance
regardless of choices.

there are moments when i wonder
whether i shall ever abide there again. there
are times when all that history
seems a far-off fantastical parade. but
there are dreams and tugs and passions that
often arise to threaten to
carry me back, and i know
it is where my spirit will remain.

Aug 28 10

visiting

i no longer hear my parents' voices
a tone perhaps
an inflexion round a smile
: but nothing clear

their faces, still
more in death now than in life:
is this what's meant by
letting go?

one sister just turned 70
one just underwent
major heart surgery:
i feel my aches and pains and know
the shock of becoming old.

the southern wind howls in around us:
my daughter and her mother tucked
warm inside the bleakness of
this wild landscape
and i contemplate the knowledge that
she one day will own
: how it will seem so very long ago.

Oct 18 11

Tia

the old dog
has perhaps days to die:
despite the steroids that
should give her appetite
(and certainly helped add some
last minute zip) tonight
she not only won't eat but
got up and moved away from her food
: with labradors, that's
a crucial sign.
now she just lays there like
a furred black log
not even bothering to twitch
the stupid hastings flies away.
there's nothing we can do
save give her extra pats and gentle caresses
trying to avoid the tumorous bulge
protruding out from her insides
: nothing the vet could do either.
tomorrow or the next day i'll
ring about a home-call put-down
: the least we can do, sparing
the anxiety of a final fraught trip.
and then, i guess, there'll be nothing but memories
to flood in like the tide every time we walk along a beach
to shuffle like the bushes every time we stroll around a park
to dip and soar like the swallows every time we picnic by a river
and catch ourselves guiltily wondering at the silence
whenever the gate creaks open.
good old dog. there's a girl. home to rest, soon now.

March 30 13

one line from rob

fight scrap scrape and bleed
drop cover hold and shake
you don't eat well from the book of life
if you make one little mistake
getting born beneath the wrong blanket
getting taught to play the wrong tune
slapped upside down on the wrong side of town
and fucked with a silver spoon
you can fight scrap scrape and bleed
but you won't get an eye for an eye
and the moneyed men will still steal the handles
off the coffin on the day you die

fight scrap scrape and bleed
drop cover hold and quake
you don't need to read if you can see
what's between the lines is fake
making moves that make you money
making grooves that make you slave
beat up each night in a two-dollar fight
is a hard way to the grave
you can drop cover hold and hope
but that's the sum of your choice
cause the devil in the detail makes damn sure
to strangle a rebel voice

yeah drop scrape shake and bleed

on a treadmill one way

they'll pat your back as a jolly good chap

if you can keep it up all day

doing time for the corporations

doing time for a spitting wage

nothing to say is the price you pay

to be left with nothing to save

don't stand up straight in the morning

don't shout that rules are lies

cause the moneyed men will put a gun to your chin

and kiss your dreams goodbye

Feb 2 12

(inspired by a line from Rob Tuwhare)

ephemeral

poets
are not supposed to grow old
to feel the body's failings
to know their soul's been sold
poets are not allowed
to have regrets
to be more than shooting stars
bright and gone to their success
poets are immortal
pure and certain, fierce and bold
they do not fear their death
: they are not supposed to grow old.

May 5 14

prayer for a friend who is dying

there are no words that i can say
to keep the swollen pain at bay
save only for a moment: a smile
a laugh a memory
remembrance of the times
that used to be when
you were fully live.
no comfort save a hand held tight
in the dark that precedes the night
though it's hard to feel our hands entwined
down the livid distance
of a telephone line.
and for all the strength that i would send
to carry you up and make you mend
there is no thing that i can do
: i cannot even die for you.
but when i hear you suffer and weep
when pain gives way to exhausted sleep
then friend i hope that you will know
and accept that now's the time to go
because
i love you so

Feb 17 15

antique

i am winding down
like an old clock
not yet a grandfather but
i could well be
not so much ticking as palpitating
not telling time so much as marking it
no longer accurate and lucky
to be right twice a day
if you wind me up i am more likely
to spring a coil than spin off the tension
my gears slip and my jewels
are tarnished and untrustworthy
and while my casing holds its secrets
the veneer is warping, badly
my face may show some wisdom but
is flyspecked and stained
in all likelihood i am well past
any guarantee of quality
soon they'll examine the maker's mark
and send me to be reclaimed

Oct 14 16

what i would have said....

clamouring swarm
eager, wanting to hear
the words the flavour the instant
they appear
seeking to hold the moment
banter on request
should it cause displeasure
it's at your behest
offstage and surrounded
i kindly shy away
there's no truth like a poet's
held at bay
drunk on aimless chatter
they think it some small test
but sometimes to hold an audience
silence is best

Jan 15 16

sorting

going through another life
one box at a time
there is so much of it! paper
words
: endless. as if
i had nothing better to do ….
trying to make sense of correspondence:
who was this person, where did they fit
: if my memory were better, i would know.
and the stories: parts
of novels, shorts, outlines
nothing i recall
: even i don't want to read them. so they go
back in the box for some ungrateful relative
to sieve through at their leisure.
much good may it do them.
the poems at least are easy
to read, though a 3-foot stack
is still daunting
: discarding them harder, despite
the sheer adolescent banality
of most.
poets, as i've observed, are not
supposed to grow old
: and this is why.

Jan 21 17

bye bye railway dreams

weeks of work demolished
in an hour:
the layout i imagined
that my sons could not. that i could
not even give away. no-one
plays with trains, these days.

little yellow-belly the shunting engine
from Santa on my tenth Christmas
speedy blue boy, the modern railcar unit
my sister sent from London when i turned eleven or twelve
and all the rest: the paraphernalia of
the enthusiastic model buff
as often as not spread far and wide across
the threadbare red carpet of the lounge
: a parental indulgence, but back then
television was a rarity and
we made our own amusements.
kept for nearly fifty years, in vain hope. but even after
dad set about constructing
the scenic layout our own house allowed
first one, then the other
showed minimal interest
and soon ignored altogether.
so, sold the lot. some good prices, some of that
vintage Triang stuff. ho HO.

and today, finally put to bin
the last of that childish dream.
guess that's how it is with children:
they take only what they want, which often as not
is not what you try to give.

April 17 18

harmony

i deal with death badly:
kicked my faithful old dog the day she died
fled my mother's hospital bed the night before
left my father with the knowledge of my second son
but did not talk to him
failed a friend who entrusted me to know his mind for his will
: i don't like it.

death makes me angry:
there is so little sense in this universe
to have it snuffed without more than a peasant's view of hope
is somewhere between mordantly unfair and unspeakably uncaring
: either way it makes me callous, too.

we've had a long relationship, death and i:
not yet as long as some, but more than many as we count it
every day another ticked off against who knows what scale
that much closer to our final meeting
: my only wish
is for death to suffer as i do.

fat chance:
i will be gone into the void
at best to wave amongst the stars, though likely unaware
at worst merely a memory
in those who once knew me, or my words, before they fade
and when that too is past, death will remain
: black, inanimate, and infinite.

Feb 15 19

absent friends

we wait
we watch
the day black, and a boy
rowing his mother out from the beach as
the fires rush in
a friend's son sending
a picture of the sun
blood-red
in a peach-coloured sky
another friend an image of smoke wisping through the trees
just beyond her back fence
yet another packed and
ready to flee their
new-built home
we watch
we wait, while they
try to deal with
this enveloping disaster
this so-predictable slow-moving apocalypse, spreading
in inexorable wind-driven waves across
the vastness of Australia
: is it irony or just desserts
that sees the country with the highest
per capita emissions
the first to burn
: our friends cannot tell. they only know
the flames of hell are encroaching, and
the long hot summer has barely begun.

Dec 31 19

when spring is far away

i watch you
walking in the park
stopping to smell the flowering trees
lilac, magnolia, admire
chinese chestnuts in bloom
. we wander
along a path the council has just made
across the grass for no
apparent reason than perhaps to stop seniors
like us
wandering too far
or to save our sensible shoes
and i wonder if
you will stay on it, or ignore it
if i am not ahead or behind or with
you.
and whether you will think
the flowers still smell as sweet
without me there.

Oct 13 20

X mars

do you want some of this?
ooh, i'll have some of that!
gimme gimme gimme it
it's mine, i want it
what'd you get?
oww! it's got spiky bits
keep that thing away from me!
look ma, real blood!
where does the battery go?
in that hole in the side, dummy
how'dja make it go?
seems to be nailed on...
awww, he doesn't do anything
well, it says there's a money-back guarantee...
the stores open again in 3 days
we can take it back then

Dec 8 20

the litterax

(in the style of Dr Seuss)

a book's a book and once it's writ

    it doesn't matter what's in it

if people want to read it, fine

    if not, that's their choice, not mine

and just because attitudes change

    is no excuse to re-arrange

the bookshelves to exclude the tome

    it's of its times, and stands alone

if we only read what we are taught

    half the books would not be bought

March 5 21

Rakiura

here
the forest speaks
in silences
rustlings
bird-song
drips
and the occasional tramp of explorers
: girls with legs right up to their waist
old men whose sturdy pins
put my feebleness to shame :
and the camaraderies
of simply being
here

busiest season ever, they say
despite the pandemic
"we're here to support our people"
the minister says
though you wonder if they need
that sentiment :
the money-machine is opposite the tinned fruit
and they've certainly got that bit
right

the water-taxis come and go
the forest broods, and
does not care
: this is how it rolls

March 27 21

asleep in Gore, 38 years on

i dream poems all night
yet do not bother to wake to record them
until i come to the root, the reason:
what was left unsaid

words are the blood and sinew
rising up to strengthen the priapus of language
so it deflowers any obstacle
: if you have any intellectual capacity
this is the hymen you must break :
crudely, words are what you fuck with
and for, and because of
what you spill from your essence in the cause of change.

no-one has the right to hold them from you
none can limit how you wield them
and when someone tells you this truth
be sure to be open to hear it.

poets gain a little infamy
when they drop this concept on a closed community
but they don't do it for that reason
: they do it because somewhere in the dross of mediocrity
staring up with moon eyes
is a boy, or girl, listening
and reinventing their world

April 7 21

there's only one forge left in the country

after the revolution
we'll all be brave and wonderful
we'll wear hemp on sundays and
knit diligently
we'll have eggs benedict without the bacon
and be lactose intolerant
we'll dye our hair with woad
and our hands with harakeke flowers and
sing like robins in the forest
: the ones you only ever catch a glimpse of

after the revolution
there'll be jam without traffic
and storms without ports to
shelter in and we'll
make do with dandelions for tea and forget
there ever was a place
called Ceylon

after the revolution we'll die
of many inglorious diseases
all made for man
and call this natural.

and when the last blacksmith working at
the last forge passes, we'll
have to dig the soil with our hands.
but we'll be happy, we few, won't
we?

May 12 21

in series

i'd rather have an orgasm than get to work on time
i'd rather sail a boat across the sea
not that i'm a sailor or can stand to not see land
but more likely work will be the death of me

i'd rather feel your heartbeat than be stuck in rush-hour traffic
i'd rather share a snuggle-space for two
not that i'm pedantic or particularly romantic
but there's only one of me and one of you

i'd rather sing a song of love than watch a rocket fly
when all the stars that are are in your eyes
even if the world is ending there's a pattern to our tending
that holds a truth when all about is lies

yes i'd rather that you held me on a darkling plain at midnight
than wept to see to see the rising of the sun
when the days are counted back, there's no doubt that we're on track
to experience the universe as one

Aug 21 21

inspired by a line from Serie Barford

memoir

i wandered off the path
a long time ago
took a fork or two
that led away from what i'd known
but no matter how far i roamed,
that road remained. it's
the way home.

i've watched as others struggled
to create their own routes for life
been distressed when they've fallen 'tween
the wheel and the knife
and seen the worth of everything
i owned
forgotten by the wayside
along the road to home.

but it barely takes a minute
to bring that passion back
to know the value of a word
to judge good from lack
and if there's anything i'd rather do
to show how much i've grown
i'd pick up my swag, and stride
a ways more down
the road to home.

Oct 15 21

from a conversation with Peter Rimmer

hey mister

here's to you, mr death
you take my friends, right and left
you take em and it makes me blue
i wish somehow death could take you

yea here's to you, you fetid fuck
how come you get all the luck?
where's the hope, the fated chance
of avoiding our macabre last dance?

and even if the rolling dice
should whisk us on to paradise
you're still the winner, blood and bone
cause dying's best done on our own

and if we sinners go to hell
i bet you're in charge there as well
finding ways to kill our souls
burning bodies, digging holes

a billion billion ways to die
with no way out, no time to cry
no memory too treasured kept
untarnished from your chilling breath

yea, here's to you, you scything cunt
in what way did we so affront
your dignity you make us pay
with coffins and memorial days

and when you cut our poor lives short
do you laugh and caper at the rort
of folk dreaming immortal songs
left to rot as you slay anon

here's to you, mr death
you take my friends, right and left
you take em and it makes me blue
i wish somehow death could take you

July 18 21

legacy

carve on rock
write on walls
etch a message with a laser
on the moon, ten miles tall

send out rockets
frozen sons
telling any they encounter how we thought
we were the chosen ones

leave a marker
fossilised bones
something to wear as pendants
or decorate the home

ours is done.
we failed.
sorry you missed us, but
we're gone.

if you can work out why
perhaps you'll have a better chance than us
to carry on

Oct 23 21

reach

i remember
holding my son in my arms
showing him the stars
making some sort of promise
suggesting there lay the future
that he might be part of.

now, my son
does not talk to me
too often the stars are obscured
by ash
and what glows instead are the embers
of civilisation.

this is how far we are fallen.

Nov 2 21

feedback

the young are savage in
their condemnation
as if experience counts for nothing
as if wisdom is not earned
they bay and bite at the least
provocation
imagining they are the champions
of the world, and none
before them has had eyes to see
or mouth to speak.

and we let them do this
being gentle in our ripostes
being humbled before their anger
being older
holding our regrets
close to our souls
wishing we had somehow had the spirit
to do more
hoping their hearts will not be broken
as ours were.
knowing they will be.

the young
are you and i, once
and we cannot but forgive them
as they refuse to forgive us
until they are older, wiser
watching new generations spoil
their memories.

without ever stopping to listen, to learn, to choose
a wider path, history repeats
because the young
are savage:
they still have all their teeth
and they bare them brightly.

Nov 3 21

cheers

i watch
as little pieces of myself
float out into the world
touching here and there
looking for shelter.

i wave them fond goodbyes
and wish their journeys will be
everything i could want
for they are my hopes
and hold my dream.

and when you say to me
i met a part of you the other day
and was nourished
then i know this work
is not in vain.

Nov 4 21

how to maintain a sense of humour

life narrows:
you spend your energy
weeding the path
worrying about the leak
in the kitchen
shuffling money around to cover
unexpected costs
and are forced to admit, when reminded, that
your latest get rich scheme is
beyond you at your age and state of health.
as are most things.

conversations repeat:
the wife's dead tooth
what happened at a friend's funeral
one drama averted and another
inescapable.
and even when
a gremlin runs across your bed
in the dead of night
you shrug off the extraordinary and
go back to sleep.

time twists:
you think it is sped up as all
the days flow by unobserved
and events of five years back become
remembered as a few months
but really it is slowing
like the battery of an electric clock
draining out the seconds
until one day it will simply stop.

this is how it is:

Dec 2 21

growing pains

my wife cares for me
as if i were 80
and frail
though i am only 66
and not yet infirm

she does it with love
and i let her, because
many days i feel 80
and many others
i become frail
and it eases us both
to know
i can go on
with a little help

long enough to pay her back
to care for her
should her mind fail
: as it may

we tease and tend and borrow
each others' strengths
and in this way
hold each other dear

Dec 11 21

being there

like lowell i had
twenty million things
to do
though i've lived most three times
as long as he
i wonder if
he did
more of them than me

i met ram dass once
when our halos intersected
he saw me as
i saw him
spare change was what
we both collected

albert said
it's all relative
and i believe that's true
though he died the day i
was born
he's here now too

Dec 27 21

in Bason's botanical garden

sitting
in a lovers garden
surrounded in flowered serenity
sheltered from
the wilding winds
i let the weight of the world
drop away
and my soul
is nourished.

this is what i need, i realise
: nature, lightness, calm :
i have lived beyond despair
and now
wish only to heal
myself.
whether the world can be healed, too, is no longer
my concern
: it is up
to those who come next
to try to do more than simply
repeat
and if i am weak to now give way
then so it is
for i must reclaim my spirit.

April 21 22

another casualty of the pandemic

when we get there
Parihaka is closed
the pa bottled up
for the duration
Taranaki too is closed
: oh, he comes out
teasingly brief
to greet the day
then retreats again into
his kakahu of cloud
as if in sympathy with
my sorrow:
 i only wanted
to stand upon the ground
to pay homage to a hero
to respect the dead by leaving
at the door
an old poem written
on first learning the full extent
of the tragedy
: but none of this i do
for the pa is off-limits
to tauiwi like me
and i resist invading
to ask.
perhaps that is why
there is neither road sign
nor site marker
nor monument
: Parihaka is closed
and keeps its own peace.

April 24 22

inheritance

you were such a caring, loving boy
when you were small
i don't know what happened
to sour that

was it me?

some day you will wake and realise
many things you assumed, but never asked

and if the faults were mine, still
we'll never know the how or why
if you let the chance
go by

i sorrow for you, on that day
weep to feel you weeping
down the years
for if sometime i was a fool
well, two fools can't tell a story
: only an unhappy ending.

May 4 22

choice

i don't want to die
unacknowledged
forgotten
at best a footnote in
someone else's biography
but that seems to be
my fate

what can i do? i am
too old to prance about the stage
engage the young
make the right impact:
i've done it once, though
clearly not long or well enough
and i no longer have
the energy
for a second coming

sure, with time
none of us will survive
: there are no immortal words
despite what the deified books
might insist
but that is cold comfort
as i stand still
in the light

ah, well
there it is
and there's no use
moaning about it; if i'd wished
for greater fame
i would have found it.
and i wouldn't be so glum
if i knew
my children would thank me.   May 24 22

in mem

there's a memorial in Shannon
(pop approx 1400) that lists
184 names dead
in the first world war. there were
about 900 folk in that district then
so its likely more than half the men
died.
probably - since the rule of thumb
was to put soldiers from
the same place
in the same company
- they died all together
all at once.

imagine the grief
when that news came home.

among those names
aside from the ones and twos there are
eight sets of three
likely all brothers
dead for the kings pleasure
in the trenches
and the mud.

imagine the grief.
it ripped the guts out of the place.

bloody butchery, i say
yes, the wife replies, the same
bloody butchery that still goes on today.

i think about the Ukraine, and
the mad mens hands on the buttons
and reflect
that death is never far away.

Oct 7 22

clubbing

the owner tells me
his staff think i'm
a grumpy old cunt; they're
too young to understand, but
he gets it, he says, though
i'll have to change and play good
if i want to get booked again.

the duty manager smiles when i relate this
fills my glass
with bourbon
almost to the top, adds
a dash of coke to colour the fact
charges the usual price.
we know cunts.

June 19 22

class

those at the top
believe the world owes
them a living
because all those below
pay them to be there

those at the bottom know
the world owes them nothing
because nothing is
what's left
when they have paid

those in the middle struggle
to pay and to not pay
they fight always to make
one greater than the other
and this is why they do not know
their place

July 25 22

another autobiography in five chapters
(with apologies to portia nelson)

i look up
and i see stars
i make a ladder to climb up and join them
but even as i reach to touch them
someone shakes the ladder
and i fall off

i look up and
still see stars
i make a book about them
and climb my ladder to give them the words
but the book burns
and i fall off again

i look up
the stars are still there
so i sit on the bottom step of my ladder
and sing a song to serenade them
but my voice is not strong enough
and they are indifferent

i look up
clouds have covered the stars
but i think they are still there
i would climb my ladder to find out
but someone has stolen it
and i don't have the energy
to make another

i no longer look up

Aug 11 22

another april fool

some nights
for no reason
loneliness steals in
maybe it's because the moon
is low
maybe it's
the autumnal chill
maybe it's just that it's late
and i'm thinking of
my children
and how little some of them
know me.

maybe i'm just sad because
the world is ending
faster than expected
: well, faster than most expected; me
i always had 2025 in mind
as a date to beware
and that seems right:
or maybe
it's my nature
and the way of poets
to be blue in order to be clear
though this feeling is
more of a fug
than a brightness.

yeah, but i've a dry house to sleep in
a wife to snuggle next to
and plenty of food in the pantry
so
maybe i should just shut the fuck up
and wither away
politely.

April 1 23

census day

this census day i'm counting myself
as someone becoming
proactive
toward
life.

i thought to start with a walk
around the block, extending
around Cornwall Park, as
briskly as reasonable
and since the sun
is out this plan
can't be foiled.

then, ignoring the computer and
its endless video distractions, i
might potter in the garden
removing that dying hydrangea
taking the nets off the strawberries
and for variation adding
the last coat of green
to the back-porch awning frame.

perhaps, if there's time or the weather
turns, i might
finally
begin to sort through my stamp collection
: you know, that thing i was always going to do
in my retirement:
if only to see
what i can easily sell
to help repair things.

or (a random wayward thought) i could
explore the benefits of
meditation
in the classical sense
instead of just daydreams
and see if any insights
pop out.

but now i've sat down to write this
and haven't mentioned smoking
and where's my second cuppa?
and it's awfully bright out there
so
perhaps i'll just count myself lucky
and call that a day.

                                                Mar 7 23

a misremembered fragment caught before sleep

who could go with me
as i turn to dust
who would hold my hand
as i do as i must
who might comfort me
that i should trust
to bear my soul

we live alone
let's not pretend
all things familiar now
will certain end
the laws that matter
will not bend
to bear my soul

yet at the crux of it
all is light
weaving through space
piercing the night
mayhap some thread of mine
will still shine bright
and bear my soul

May 28 23

blink and you'll miss it

when's the election?
when when when?
i hope it's soon
i can't wait!
time to get it moving
time to do it for real
stand up for what matters and
make this country better than before
yes!

oh, yay! they won!
hurrah!
now we'll show em
now we'll get ahead
all those losers with their hang-dog looks
and tales between their legs
had best watch out!
yea
our boys and girls have got their number
they'll see us right

o, hey
what's happening?
nothing seems to have changed
they're going round in circles!
this is not what i voted for
where are all their pretty promises?
where's the actual action?
gosh, i hate to say it, but
they're almost as bad
as the last lot!

don't you people care?

June 30 23

remembering Nambassa et al

"i am the knife
i cut i slice i contrive..."

that's how i'd start
in the old days
ranting and carving across
any stage, and you
would be held spellbound
by a fool come to town

but now the blade
is rusty
and even were it sharp the body
lacks the oomph to give it
full effect
: or so i tell myself

if you want comedy, son, it's
down the road
i bear too many scars
to be easy in
fulfilling your lack
and that's not the dream
that gets me up
on a line
in the morning

"i am the whole damn globe, rent asunder
i am the master, and the slaves who pass under..."

yea, verily
it has come to pass

we are all slaves
because it didn't last
that spark that saw
perhaps a hundred thousand of us
grokking together back
in '79

: where are you now? in which part
of the machine have you hidden your shine?

the light may still seep out, on occasion
but the eyes of those
who think themselves newly awake
are closed to it.

these days to cause trauma
i choose a blunt-force instrument
though it does little good when you already
suffer concussion
and i am a blood-letter
not a healer

July 2 23

linda

my wife is tender-hearted
she cares so much for the world
people places animals situations
that her heart
fills with grief
when she cannot heal them.

in part i blame myself: i
opened her eyes to politics, and
where once she held herself
aloof from such pettiness
and steered a care-free course
now she stews at the dross and savagery
we witness, daily.

she berates herself, thinking
(as some close to her have
cruelly intimated) that
it is a type of vanity
a self-indulgence
to express a want to help
but the truth is simply
that she cares
: and i love her for it.

i would like to take away
or shield her from
the grief
but we both know that the world is as it is

and to live a hermetic life
to shut it out
would not stop its churning.

besides, she knows while such isolation
might offer ease
in some ways it would cripple
both of us: me, because i
need to know; her,
because she needs community.

even if it spurns her. so
she seals away the hurt
and continues to care
though she cries sometimes for
no other reason
and i can only kiss the tears away
and hold her close
and extend my condolences.

that seems to be as much as we can do.

July 31 23

    that pretty much sums it up

i go to a funeral
the day before i start treatment
: glad it's not
the other way around:
and find myself contemplating
the god particle as
a sweet spring breeze
twirls through
the cemetery
wishing i knew the words
to how great thou art in te reo
so i could join in.

babies gurgle and toddlers
slap about in gumboots
while an older man sharing
an outdoor seat with me seems surprised
the deceased - a Vietnam vet - wasn't
older than his 81. contrary,
i thought he looked
ten years younger.
but the fellow is
a good twenty years my senior, so should
be a better judge.

surprised, too, at how many vets
there are kicking about
plus those sending condolences from
afar. these are men
who went through war
yet have held up
remarkably well.

i consider the way the dice roll
decide if any gods are present they
are keeping a low profile. then explain
to a hulking young man - 6'3", with
size 14 feet he complains about - how
the cremation process works.
hope it's cleaned out well, he says; hate to be
mixed up with someone else.

Oct 17 23

here we go

i watch an old friend
having fun
playing and singing as if
he had no cares. he still
looks reasonably well - within the range
age leaves us. but i know
he has stage 4 bone cancer
and is on borrowed time
even though his meds are
keeping him stable
for now.

i'm fortunate enough
to be able to get up and sing a song
with his band, and get
many good compliments for it, but i wonder
how much of a tune i'd carry
if our positions
were reversed.

hopefully, when
my test results come back in
a couple of weeks,
they won't be.

August 27 23

    well, bully for you

the bully boys wear corporate ties
tailored suits on their porcine thighs
tell you truths that are downright lies
and expect you to admire them.

the bully girls look down their nose
line up their dolls in military rows
fall on the poor like a murder of crows
and expect you to desire them.

the bully nation rolls its sleeves
plays at care like it's disease
keeps its workers on their knees
just where it wants them.

the bully boys, the bully girls,
the bully nation in a whirl
sliding off the edge of the world
taking you with them.

Sept 26 23

a familiar tune

wake up in the morning kill a palestinian
wish that every one can be dead
oh, oh, the israelites

they've nowhere to run but still we give a warning
so we're not called war criminals instead
oh, oh, the israelites

missiles on their houses, missiles on their hospitals
bombs on the baker who makes their daily bread
oh, oh, the israelites

cut off all their water gas and electricity
and blame their leaders so you will be misled
oh, oh, the israelites

if they shoot at us we stage a big reprisal
and keep on killing no matter how they beg
oh, oh, the israelites

there's no irony in what we're doing
genocide's the way we've made our national bed
oh, oh, the israelites

woe woe woe
oh, oh, the israelites...

Nov 7 23

    how we missed the war

when everything was usual
where anything could be saved
when sirens were only warnings
and memory marked the graves

when countries were still countries
and not corporates in drag
where you might still die trying
yet have reason to be glad

when even three-cornered governments
distinguished means from end
where reason had equality
and faith wasn't part of the spend

oh, how we missed it
for look where it's brought us now
wrapped in a comforting encore
too numb for a final bow

too mad to even be sorry
too dumb to even show fear
swapping bright forever instants
in the galloping cancer of here

Nov 19 23

in camp cancer

the roses are flowering
in camp cancer
the inmates regard the blooms
and try to ignore their thorns
soon the harsh south-west wind
will scatter the petals
as we, collected here, are scattered
perhaps to live
perhaps to return
in a season closer to our fall.

Nov 23 23

SONGS

(bruce's blues)

Heavens Road   (jaunty country bop)

I've been a traveller / all round this place
I've been to the bottom / I've been disgraced
I've been where the preacher / told me I'd go
But now I'm walkin on heavens road

I am a poor man / one shirt no tie
I don't regret it / my life's no lie
But I've had fortunes / if it was not gold
And now I'm walkin on heavens road

CH:

On heavens road, on heavens road
Yes I'm happy just to be on heavens road
That man done pick me up
And made me whole
That's why I'm walkin on heavens road

I am a sinner / I called it fun
I been the first in line / when sinnin's done
I can't remember / all the debts I owe
But now I'm walkin on heavens road

I ain't afeared / I'm not in pain
I don't believe I'll be / cast out again
I've seen my future / and when the story's told
They'll say he rose up and walked down heavens road

CH X 2

Verse: F/F/C/C F/F/C/G F/F/C/Am C*/G/C/C
Chorus: F/F/C/C F/F/G/G C/C7/F/F# C/G/C

Take This Heart   (slow, melodic)

i been down this road before
i hung round outside love's door
i said sorry, i begged for more
but i believe i still can't say what this heart's for

i promised you life, i promised truth
i promised a helping hand to see you through
i built a homeland on a desert shore
but i believe i still don't know what this heart's for

and all those girls who were untrue
keep on haunting me with unpaid dues
i cry i pledged my soul, they wanted more
and i just can't believe they didn't know what this heart's for

take this heart, set it free
let the spring of love well up in me
unchain my sorrow, stop this war
let me find the one who knows what this heart's for

now i've found the one who knows what this heart's for

July 23 92

(2 verses in B, 1 in F, 1 in G)

C/C/C/G/C/F/C/G/C x2

F/F/F/C/F/Bb/F/C/F x2 (inc break)

G/G/G/D/G/C/G/D/G/G/D/C/G

Song for Ralph (One Time)   (jaunty, upbeat)

Ch:
One time I made a mistake
One time I baked the cake
One time that's all it takes
Just one time to seal my fate

The man was short on my usual supply
I wanted a kick, I needed a high
So I bought me a trip to the dark of the moon
With a used needle and a silver spoon

(Ch)

35 years til it bit me back
Pain in my liver like an acid attack
I asked the doctor, please tell me why
He said I'm sorry son but you're gonna die

(Ch)

Now I don't regret the things I've done
The kids I've made and the songs I've sung
But if I had the chance again, I do believe
I wouldn't share the needle with my worst enemy

(Ch)

G/E/C/D x2

G/G7/C/Cm/G

-- Feb 2015

I heard the gospel gotcha

When the time comes
When the time comes
Gonna take you up by hand when the time comes
Gonna play that steel guitar all across the promised land
When the time comes

When the moon's high (x2)
Gonna pass on down that road singing bye and bye
Gonne dare to meet his eye and lose that heavy load
When the moon's high

When the star shines (x2)
Gonna pack away your blues and leave this world behind
Gonna taste the fruit divine and wear your dancing shoes
When the star shines

When the time comes (x2)
Gonna heed the angels' calls from up above
Won't mind eternity cause paradise is where you'll be
When the time comes

Yes, gonna play that steel guitar all across the promised land
When the time comes….

June 6 15

Slow, melodic; piano: A (played as diad, just E & A), E7, D7

guitar: C/G/Am/F

Local yokel festival blues   (tex/mex hop)

We went to play the festival, we got added to the bill
Cause you know folk like to boogie even when they're from the hill
But when we went to set up we found out there was a catch
We got hi-brow arts on here, they said, so you have to play out back

There's a woman playin violin and singin torchy songs
A couple being cultural while writing up a storm
And another with a one-gal play who doesn't want no noise
But we know you'll grin and bear it, won't ya boys

ch:
They said you're down in the dust
You playin down in the dust
You boys is just musicians
So you shouldn't get too fussed
Out back by the barbecue
We've got a patch of sand
And that's the only place to put a band

Well Jules he started tappin ... Tony riffled up his bass
Then Lennie got his slide a-glidin right up into space
Pete boogied on the ivories and when BB opened wide
The blues rolled out across the whole damn site

Them arty types is wiser now they've seen what we can do

They stomped and hollered til they cried and tossed back more than a few

And every girl and her sidekick got dirtier than planned

When they got down in the dust with our blues band

ch:

They said you're down in the dust

You playin down in the dust

You boys is just musicians

don't expect too much

Out back by the barbecue

We've got a patch of sand

And that's the only place for your blues band

Oct 18 18

Verse: Gb x6/ A/ D   G6 G7 C Cm G E D G

Chorus: C9 / C9 / etc

Old man blues

I saw an old man sittin by himself
Starin into space the way they do
He looked like he could use some cheerin up
So I said hey pop why you feelin blue

Well he looked at me as if I wasn't there
Then he coughed a little round a sigh
He said son you haven't got the faintest clue
What it's like to get too old before you die

CH:
Boy, you're gonna get lonely
All your friends will pass you by
Take a tip from one who knows it
Don't get old before you die

He said I used to dream about growin old
Havin all my family round
I never thought that they would leave me here
Or that my wife would be asleepin in the ground

All the good times are just memories
Of someone I suppose I used to be
So sonny if its all the same to you
Just go your way and leave me be

CH
Coda:
We don't know what some folk mean to us
Til we try to fill the spaces when they're gone
So if you have someone who's dear to you
Try not to leave them singing this sad song

CH

Dec 23 18

E A / E B7 / E A / E B7 E   mid-paced

When I fall   (slow, melodic)

sometimes love is scattered by the mistakes that we make
sometimes love is shattered when the truth arrives too late
sometimes love revolves as we evolve toward our fate
and sometimes love will catch you when you fall

sometimes there's a loneliness that cannot stand the heat
sometimes there's an only-ness that refuses the beat
sometimes there's a place where every trace of freedom's sweet
and sometimes love will catch you when you fall

ch:
maybe there's a pain inside that never goes away
a feeling close to self-denied for all your yesterdays
if you feel that hurt won't heal then all I have to say
is sometimes love will catch you when you fall

most of us have moments when we look the other way
most of us have torments when we decide not to stay
we often hide our voices to make choices come what may
but sometimes love will catch us when we fall

every day's a cycle from the sun unto the moon
every moment's fickle when the world is crying doom
every breath is even til you walk into the room
yea sometimes love will catch you when you fall

ch:
now the wind is calling and the silver moon is high
my spirit feels like soaring to that castle in the sky
but the ground's a long way down when you've forgotten how to fly
I hope your love will catch me when I fall

yes, I hope your love will catch me
I hope your love will catch me
I hope your love will catch me when I fall

-- 2020

Verse:

A G G A
A G A G
A G G A
A G A G

Chorus:

D C D C
D C C B♭
D C C-B♭ A
A G A

Endword

Well, there we are. The bits that got captured the last 40 years. And why, I presume to hear you ask, has it been so long since my third book, "Coming Up Hard", came out in 1983? Because after several years on the road I gave up performing c.1986... and since performing is half the art - I could do a long diatribe about that, but suffice to say IT IS! - there was no sense publishing if I wasn't performing more than on odd occasion.

What's changed? Age, in short. I kept writing, and the stack kept mounting... but while I may be able to still do a few turns round various stages I now lack energy to do that most of the time. So I've accepted that to reach an audience it must be via this half-arsed method; my apologies but you'll have to imagine the voice and the swagger. Though I hope something of both comes through.

Poetry must be simple to read, in both senses: crucially, aloud, because poetry began as oratory and song and, as Jorge Luis Borges reminded us, **must** be spoken - which is why I write in "breathlines". But also as in easy to understand, for the audience is the world and much of it is not "lettered"; obscure language only works if it can readily be interpreted from what surrounds. And like any art, poetry must be able to communicate with whoever encounters it - else it fails in its purpose. So, simple is best.

The poems (and songs) presented were as usual for me all written on the instant; if they have flaws, well, that's how they came - spontaneous crafting is tricky.

As for the title, apart from the obvious it also bookends my first volume, "beginnings" (pub. 1979). Is it actually my last published word? Not if you count the odd poem popping up on the internet... but in print, who knows? Best however to assume so.

That just leaves me to thank former laureate and ranter David Eggleton for graciously agreeing to cull and weed the stack to derive the contents herein, my luscious photographer friend Petra Zoe for the cover design, and long-time supporter of weirding voices Michael O'Leary for allowing me to publish under his imprint. And of course you, for buying this.

I'll finish by reiterating that since I write for performance, the poems should be READ ALOUD.

-- Bruce Bisset, Hastings / Heretaunga, 2024.

BIOGRAPHICAL NOTES:

Bruce Bisset is a sixth-generation pakeha who was born in the Waikato, grew up in Auckland, made his home on Waiheke Island and now lives in Hastings (Hawke's Bay). He is a poet who has also been a journalist, corporate video writer/director, blues singer, environmental activist and newsletter editor, film & video technicians' guild co-ordinator, café/venue owner/manager (twice), elected local body politician (3 terms), and newspaper columnist.

He spent 1979-1985 living as a professional performance poet, spending most of each year touring the length and breadth of New Zealand and performing on everything from random bar tables to Nambassa's main stage, including three national high schools' tours, with and alongside a wide range of the country's musical and poetic talent.

His published work includes the self-published volumes "beginnings" (1979), "Explanation and other poems" (1980), and "Coming Up Hard" (1983). He also featured in the iconic 2-book-and-tape collection "The Globe Tapes" (Hard Echo Press, 1985).

Other works include a fantasy novel, "Under Duress" (self-pub. via Amazon, 2020) - with more in the series to come.

Recordings include "Air Aces Live" (cassette tape, with Ralph Bennett, 1983) and "Air Aces Live Revisited" (cassette tape, with Bennett and Taranaki Sol, 1984); and "Unfenced and Rawboned" (CD, Bruce Bisset & the Rural Voters, 2020).

CONTACT:

Email: booksalesnz@gmail.com
Website: brucebisset.com

The good old days... Bruce Bisset with Ralph Bennett, 1980

Advance Reviews of "endings" :

These poems connect us to the real: love, fatherhood, politics, war, nationhood, passing time, matters of heart and mind. There is melancholy here, a rueful humour and ruthless honesty. As the poems unfold you can feel the rhythm and cadence of a lifetime passing by with its triumphs and regrets as the world slips deeper into disaster and the years take their toll on faith and hope. These accessible, straight from the shoulder poems morph easily into song. They teeter on the edge of despair but 'Sometimes love will catch you when you fall.'

-- Mike Johnson - writer, poet, publisher

www.ingramcontent.com/pod-product-compliance
Lightning Source LLC
Chambersburg PA
CBHW050255120526
44590CB00016B/2356